YOUR KNOWLEDGE HAS VALUE

- We will publish your bachelor's and
  master's thesis, essays and papers

- Your own eBook and book -
  sold worldwide in all relevant shops

- Earn money with each sale

Upload your text at www.GRIN.com
and publish for free

Junaid Javaid

Personal & Professional Development (PDP)

GRIN Verlag

Bibliografische Information der Deutschen Nationalbibliothek:

Die Deutsche Bibliothek verzeichnet diese Publikation in der Deutschen National-
bibliografie; detaillierte bibliografische Daten sind im Internet über http://dnb.d-
nb.de/ abrufbar.

Imprint:

Copyright © 2012 GRIN Verlag GmbH
Druck und Bindung: Books on Demand GmbH, Norderstedt Germany
ISBN: 978-3-656-74821-2

This book at GRIN:

http://www.grin.com/en/e-book/281116/personal-professional-development-pdp

PERSONAL & PROFESSIONAL DEVELOPMENT (PDP)

ASSESSMENT-1

WRITTEN & SUBMITTED BY:
JUNAID JAVAID

DATE OF SUBMISSION:
23-NOVEMBER-2012

Table of Contents

1. Executive Summary

This report is written on the topic 'Personal and Professional Development' which was introduced by University of Bedfordshire's former student named Arti Kumar. In term of scope this report is broader in context as it includes the application and utilization of certain frameworks and model which we read and learnt in Business Communication module 2. This report consists of two main sections (Findings & Conclusion). In the finding phase, I applied the SOAR model for the purpose of career development. This SOAR framework has four aspects which are: Self awareness, Opportunities, Aspirations and Results. In the first factor (Self-Awareness) I applied another model called MAP (Motivation, Ability and Personality) and found that the career progression is my prominent motivating factor and also concluded that the learning style which looks most attracting for myself is Diverger. And at last I also determined that the personality type characteristics which carried is Harmoniser. In the opportunity phase, I sorted out that in the short run, the most feasible option for myself is to engage in UK retail sector through the temporary or part time job and while in the long run, It would most attracting thing for me is to get employment in the Libyan Government sector as my preference is Job security when it comes to evaluate and analysis any job position. So it means that my aspiration is get employed by Government and then to progression in the specified department or area. Then in the Result phase, I demonstrates the result by mentioned that I have crafted my CV and Cover Letter in relation to the Aspirations I outlined in the previous part. After the SOAR model, I used and harnessed some more models to explore and elaborate self-relisation in depth. Through the use of Johari Window Test on Internet, I discovered certain new things about myself that my blind spot characteristics are intelligent, mature, extrovert and caring. And while the open Area traits are Trustworthy and Confident. Through undergoing Cash-flow Quadrant model, I determined that as job security is my prominent approach in evaluating the given job, so I want to engage myself in Employee Quadrant in short-run as well as in long-run. At the very end, I used Covey's 7 Habits theory and preferred to adopt first three habits as it will be enough to me to have to do the government job. So, one can say that this report summarises all my career planning and development.

2. Introduction

This report basically describes my UK's journey through the use of SOAR & MAP model. The report comprises of two section findings and conclusion. In the finding phase, I use SOAR model on my own-self. As you know SOAR is consisting of four factors (Self awareness, Opportunities, Aspirations and Results), so it will assist me to understand where I'm know and where I want to be in future. Within the Self-Awareness aspect I have also another model called MAP (Motivation, Ability & Personality) in order to navigate through my career's journey. In the second aspect (Opportunity), I will mention the all available options which can I avail in either short or long run and all this is possible through the Opportunity Structure Theory. In third phase (Aspirations), I will give explanation about my career aspiration which is to be made on SMART (Specifiable, Measureable, Achievable, Realistic & Time-Restricted) objectives. And in the final phase of SOAR model, I will show the results which is made in the form of Action Plan, I have developed to achieve the objectives and aspirations in the long-run.

Then afterward, I will use Johari Window in order to identify the traits carried by my-self including the open area and blind spot. I will used another model called cash-flow quadrant to analyze that which quadrant is most important for me from the career development point of view and then in last I will use Covey's 7 Habits model to evaluate which habit should I adopt for the purpose career preparation and development.

3. Findings

In this section, various models will be applied to get detailed information about the career planning and the career development. The list of model which will used is mentioned below:

- SOAR Model (Framework)
- MAP Model
- Johari Window
- Cash-Flow Quadrant
- Covey's 7 Habits

These models are briefly discussed and explained below.

3.1. SOAR FRAMEWORK

This framework was introduced by University of Bedfordshire's former student named as Arti Kumar. This model is made up of four important components (Kumar, 2008); each component is explained and applied in the section afterward.

3.1.1. Self-Awareness

According to the Arthor (Arti Kumar) the 'Self' component is the central and the crucial factor in the SOAR model as it not only helps in acknowledging self-awareness but also helps in getting awareness about other skills as well.

In order to analyze how I approach and reach goals (Self Efficacy), I have used Goal Setting Theory. In result of this theory, I managed to make four propositions which are listed below:

a) I will set challenging goals for the purpose of performance enhancement.

b) My performance will be enhanced.

c) My commitments towards attaining goals will be increased.

d) Feedback in the result of overall performance will helps myself in numerous ways.

After using Self-Efficacy, I went towards using Self-mapping which is made up of three pillars (Motivation, Ability and Personality type). For the purpose of MAP, I have undergone certain psychometric test mentioned on the Job Savvigrad's extra feature called Profiling for Success. And all MAP results are generated through all those tests.

3.1.1.1. Motivation

i. Through conduction activities like 'My Journey through Life' and other related activities, I discovered that I believe on my strength and I'm really much aware about all options available to me. So this thing would helps me in Continuous Profession Development.

ii. By undergoing Career Inventory test, I found out that the career in which I'm really much interested is the Occupation of Enterprising.

iii. The output created in result of Values Inventory test suggests me that the factor which is be valued for me in evaluating any type of job is the career progression.

iv. Evidence: The results are to be the true reflection of my aspiration which are to be known as the preference being made in attaining any goal in the given time frame.

3.1.1.2. *Ability*

i. By undergoing Dynamic Type indicator work test, I found out that I have various abilities:

- In harmonious and co-operative working atmosphere, I can work efficiently.
- I have ability to work in the organizations based on task-orientation.
- I can manage and control multi-tasking role.
- I can perform well in the pressure situations.

ii. By using Kolb Learning test, I determined that the learning style which suits my capabilities and essentials is Derverger and further discover certain traits:

- I find out to be an entertaining thing to work on complex problems and likewise to suggest innovative solution for the given problem or issue.
- For the better understanding, I love to explore and relates certain theories,
- I love to acquire knowledge which is possible through the research, reading or critical evaluation and thinking.

iii. Evidence: the learning preferred by myself is diverger as I love to work in the organizations which are to be known as task orientation and have adopted Management By Objective (MBO) approach.

3.1.1.3. *Personality*

i. Through the MBTI personality type indicator test, I came to know that Harmoniser (ESFJ) is my personality type which is made-up of four facets (Extrovert, Sensing, Feelings and Judgment). And also drawn the conclusion that the job needed by me will be of nature which promotes goodwill and co-operation extensively.

ii. By indulging in Belbin exercise, I discover that the role which suits me under team performance is the role of team player which shows that I'm a caring person and always try myself to avoid and resolve conflicts arises within the team I'm working for.

iii. Evidence: Throughout my study and professional career, I always try my best to avoid conflicts with the team as it would effects the team effectiveness and team efficiency.

3.1.2. Opportunity

It is the second most important aspect of SOAR framework as it helps students like me to extract and look for most attractive option for them which will helps in shaping the whole career in a gentle manner.

By undergoing Wheel of opportunity, I understood that I have variety of options available as I can choose to go for Doctorate Degree or to engage myself in the UK's retail sector for the short period of time. While in the long-run I have an option to start my-own business or to get employment in Libyan Government Sector.

3.1.3.   Aspiration

Aspiration deals with the decisions associated the student's career development. It is important to have aspiration as it is the hope or one person's motivating factor towards accomplishing his/her core objective. That is why Arti Kumar called Aspirations as Career Development Learning (CDL). Basically the aspirations formulates, attested, implemented and adjusted on the basis of previous to aspects (Self-Awareness and Opportunity).

My aspiration in the short-run is to get employment in UK's retail company (TESCO, ASDA or Sainsbury), in order to grab some experience and learning which will enable to share the acquired knowledge with the friends living in my home country and likewise will giving me an edge over other applicants when I attach that experience on my CV.

While in the long-run, I want to look myself on the government post as It will not only cover up the job security aspect but also will be great honors for my family members as well who always wants to look me on good position and I think government job is not a bad option in this regard.

Below I have listed the action plan as guided by Arti Kumar:

My main long-term goal My long-term objective is to occupy good position in any government sector.	**To be achieved by:** I must attain this MSc Finance Degree as It will enhance the chances of getting the job I'm being desired for.
My Short-term goals My short-term goal is to get employed in any UK's retail store (ASDA, Sainsbury or TESCO) in order to get the experience of working in Supermarket giants.	**To be achieved by:** I have to apply online on the retail stores website by submitting my CV. I can go for another option by registering with specified recruitment agencies appointed by these stores.
Action Steps: How am I going to achieve this?	

- I have to get MSc Finance Degree.
- Do the jobs in the retail market up to the expiration my visa permit.
- Keep an eye on the vacancies open for Libyan Government especially in the finance sector.
- Go back to Home County.
- Attend the interview in-person.

Table 1 Action Plan, adapted from Kumar (2008)

Task/stages involved	Resources/people who can help	Time-scale
1. Attain MSc Finance Degree.	Hard-work and Capabilities.	1 year
2. Do part-time job in UK	Recruitment Agencies and University's Career Department.	1-2 year
3. Keep on applying for Libyan Government Vacancy.	IT Skills	1-2 year
4. Go back to home country.	Home Office	2 year
5. Do job at the desired post.	My skills, knowledge and abilities.	2-10 year

Table 2 Action Plan-2, adapted from Kumar (2008)

3.1.4.   Result

The result demonstration is forth component of SOAR model and also the last initiative towards Career Orientation through the development and enhancement of skills for the purpose of professional career development.

For this aspect, I have made the CV and Cover Letter according to the set format directed by the University. These documents will be used as central instrument in searching or applying for any desired job. So, one can say that with the use of SOAR model I'm able to align my job preferences with the type of personality traits inherent in myself. And according this feature Arti Kumar named Result aspect as the common denominator.

3.2. JOHARI WINDOW

This model is used extensively for the purpose of self-awareness from the individual point of view (West & Turner, 2011). But the in the corporation it is being used to identifying personality differences among their employees or among the applicants who are being interviewed to analyse that either the given employee or applicant is matched to the given job description and also to the job specification with an intention of appointing right person at the right place.

The figure below shows the result of my Interactive Johari Window test:

	Known to Self	Not Known to Self
Known to Others	**Common Area** confident trustworthy	**Blind Spot** caring extroverted intelligent mature
Not Known to Others	**My Secrets** introverted knowledgeable self-conscious	**Unconscious-Self** able accepting adaptable bold brave calm cheerful clever complex dependable dignified energetic friendly giving happy helpful idealistic independent ingenious kind logical loving modest nervous observant organised patient powerful proud quiet reflective relaxed religious responsive searching self-assertive sensible sentimental shy silly spontaneous sympathetic tense warm wise witty

So the above result shows the good characteristics which I carried with my personality. While for the purpose of identifying bad aspects of my personality traits, I must go for the Nohari Window. But on the general level, I'm quite happy with the outcomes generated in result of that test.

3.3. CASH-FLOW QUADRANT

The Cash-flow Quadrant model was proposed by Robert Kiyosaki for three reasons (Kiyosaki & Lechter, 1999), listed below:

- Identification of Individual recent quadrant.
- Directing and distinguishing towards quadrants which have financial freedom like Investor and Businessman or those which have job security such as Self-Employed or Employee.

- What type of skills an individual should develop to be categorized or listed in the desired quadrant.

The whole picture of Cash-Flow quadrant model is depicted below:

Figure 1 Cash-flow Quadrant, adapted from Richard West & Lynn H. Turner (2006)

As I already mentioned in the SOAR model that the most attracting thing for myself which I analysed during job evaluation is the Job Security and also mentioned that my aspiration is to work for the government organization for the long period of time. So I will definitely go for Employee Quadrant and hope to achieve continuous career progression in the related field.

3.4. COVEY'S 7 HABITS

This model shows the level of effectiveness an individual must work and adopt to complete the given tasks. So for this purpose an individual has to development certain habit in one own-self to achieve the level of effectiveness required by the given job or role. For this Covey has mentioned 7 habits (Covey, 2004) under three different levels, which are mentioned below:

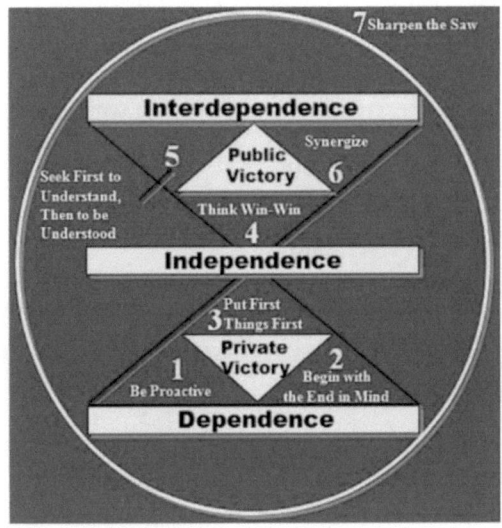

As you government job requires dependence as most of the time the Authority is hold only by the executive position, so it will be best for me to adopt and follow first 3 habits which come under Dependence Level.

4. Conclusion

The conclusion drawn from the report is that the SOAR and MAP models important for both purpose Self-Awareness and Career Development. It's not only a self assessment tool but also guide one person how he/she can align his/her job preferences with the characteristics incorporated in their personality type. With the result generated form Johari Window test, I'm very much aware my known and unknown good traits. While on the hand, I discover that with the use of cash-flow quadrant that I must stay at the Employee Quadrant for the purpose of job security and active income. And by the last model, I understand that I should follow dependence level habits for the successful career management.

5. What I hope to achieve?

The milestones I want to accomplish are listed below:

- I want to be post-graduate student in the subject of Finance.

- I want to work at temporary basis within the retail market giants.
- I want to see myself to achieve maximum level of job position in the minimum amount of tume.
- I want to see my friends and family members to be proud about my advancement.

6. What would be the outcomes?

The forecasted outcomes are listed below:

- I would be satisfied with the achievement I accomplish in the given time-frame.
- I would advice other friends to go to UK especially for the Higher Education as It will be unforgettable experience and journey for their-selves.
- My parents would happy to admire that their expectation comes true.
- I would get recognition certificate from the Libyan Government.

7. References

Covey, S. R., 2004. *Seven Habits of Highly Effective People.* New York: Free Press.

Kiyosaki, R. T. & Lechter, S. L., 1999. *Rich Dad's Cashflow Quadrant: Rich Dad's Guide to Financial Freedom.* New York: TechPress Incorporated.

Kumar, A., 2008. *Personal, Academic and Career Development in Higher Education SOARing to Success.* London: Routledge..

Robert, K., 1977. The Social Conditions, Consequences and Limitation of Careers Guidance. *British Journal of Guidance and Counselling,* I(5), pp. 1-9.

West, R. & Turner, L. H., 2011. *Understanding Interpersonal Communication: Making Choices in Changing Times.* 3rd ed. London: Cengage.